CW00524184

First Edition.

ISBN; 9781089887935

Dearest Ronnie, Maddy, El, Billy, Pat, Indy and all the other incredible friends of yours I have recently met.

You are incredible people, you have taught me many things and quite literally been the best part of my life during these strange times.

Hopefully these are feelings you share. Let this book stay with you for a long time, to remind you of the excellent time we have had. (I am sure there is more to come).

Your friendship helped me have confidence through the worry of publishing this book. It is not perfect but I think we have learned that can be ok. Enjoy.

Lots of Love,
        James.

I dedicate my first collection
to anyone who has shared a meal with
me, of my cooking or otherwise. And
especially to my young sister Esme, who
has drawn every picture contained within
this little book.

Thanks also to the Boddington-Rees family
who lent us their beautiful home in France.
I hope this book finds a place for eternity
on your kitchen shelf.

vi

"Of course reading and thinking are important
but, my God, food is important too."
— Iris Murdoch, The Sea, The Sea

Itzac, France.

Le Maison Figues, in the countryside of the former Occitan region of modern-day *Midi-Pyrenees* will be the unifying feature of all instruction henceforth. As this house, which is named after the fig trees that apparently grew there but certainly grow no more, was where this food was first prepared and eaten in combination. The romance of the surrounding vine fields, rolling hills and superior vegetable growing conditions produces a base response in any individual concerned (or obsessed) with matters of gustatory pleasure. As a member of the latter group, the week over which these recipes were found or conceived and then recorded was one of immense enjoyment. A feeling I hope not to have lost by the end of translating my week into the artefact of a book.

The vastness and refinement of France's culinary tradition may never be captured in a small book written by an Englishman. I will attempt however to give the essence of how one may cook in France; standing in the shadows of many a generation of culinary genius. The people here eat, and drink, in a different way. Herbs are fresh from the garden; rosemary, a personal favourite of mine, is never overused because there is never a shortage; regional dishes thrive because the immense variety in growing condition. We can see this through variations in weather, produce different wines and different foods at different regions. This country borders two different seas, five mountain ranges and eight different nations. British people cannot understand this feeling, I do not claim to, but will seek to explore the foods it makes me feel like cooking. These dishes are exclusively French cuisine, some are inspired by it, but all are in some way related by my own experience, or the history of the foods concerned.

Recipe books are often inherently flawed because they sterilise the passion and improvisation that characterises cooking in a well-stocked kitchen. I will offer looser than usual instruction here as I wish readers to become accustomed to taking control of their cooking and most importantly making the most of what they have at hand. Knowledge of some cooking techniques is assumed here, but not necessary. Explanations will be given where possible and if this is not enough many instructive online guides can be found for all terms and processes that will be used. Additionally, even though some more complicated methods are mentioned, the home kitchen in France from where this collection was written is unlikely to contain equipment most people would not have at home. This should make every recipe accessible, no matter where it is being cooked from.

In rural isolation, one hours drive to the nearest *supermarché* I relied heavily on a well-stocked larder but suffered from a lack of access to all the foods I might want. The solution, a care-free approach to substituting ingredients for those that will fill their places. By identifying the role that each food plays in the construction of a dish it is possible to find others that can do the same thing. This brings minor variations that develop the nature of a meal into something it would not have been before. Hopefully this attitude will be adopted at times by those who follow through these recipes for themselves. The recipes here are not the only way to cook each dish; they are the results of my efforts to understand it. For this reason the book is not a textbook but rather a story of my education.

We are shortly before midsummers day and I hope the foods that follow will be suggestive of what was mostly outdoor dining under the fading evening sun. The book is essentially the tale of an Englishman, in France, cooking for friends. An introduction to the food that I like to eat and the time I took learning to cook it. All quantities will be given to serve four people, unless otherwise stated, as this was the number that shared the trip with me. Four is indeed the best number to cook for. Apart from two. All but a few recipes are inherently gluten free, thanks to one of our dinner guests, they are however rarely vegetarian and seldom vegan, although some could be adjusted to be so.

Le Pigeonnier, Itzac.

History.

To justify the position of a British adolescent writing a cookbook about French food as if they were a chef would be impossible. It may seem at first to be yet another sign that the traditions of both food and publishing have fallen to the hands of the uneducated mob. I would however contend that this is in fact solid evidence that dedicated people can, and should, do anything if they care about it. Should a person like me be able to become a part of literary food history then we must live in a good place in time where it is safe and possible to do all the things we enjoy.

The history of food and food writing is long, 'foodies' as they are now known (I am not one, this is a ridiculous term), have continually been questioned for why they are obsessed with decadent consumption: one of the seven deadly sins. Surely an individual should care more to help people or produce good for the world. Plutarch, a Roman historian, wrote that a being concerned too much with the stomach and not the mind was the mark of a slave – so clearly this concern has been around for a while. In France, and indeed most of Europe until very recently, cooking was not a popular pastime. People cooked only as a means of sustenance from what food they could find. As societies grew and some people became rich, servants would create feasts for their masters but receive little acclaim for their work. Eventually, a small handful of cookbooks were written, slowly the worlds interest in its eating habits grew. However, the majority of the population, poor, still ate little. Many women stayed at home to cook for working husbands until the last century when, with the growth of the consuming classes, the same husbands started buying mass printed cookbooks and people began going out to eat. Many individuals are now interested in creating high quality food at home - because they can.

I will jokingly argue that our personal position in this history gives us access to the most deeply evolved recipes, foods and attitudes to eating in the world. Living at the end of the line of a long history of foods development, from hand ground bread and gathered berries to Sunday lunch feasts with any food you desire. For better or worse, readers of this text must acknowledge their advantage. Many people of the past and present did not have time or do not have money to satisfy the tastes we have developed. Nevertheless, amongst peers there is a responsibility shared to develop further what knowledge and tastes already exist and to share the pleasures we can enjoy.

To understand my evolutionary argument for how Britain is so excellently placed to experience the best cuisine and recipes in history, one must accept a mildly deterministic and under-researched socio-ecological account of the history of homo-sapiens and their nourishment. Which is clearly depicted in the dad's army style diagram below. Since the dawn of mankind in the fertile crescent, all great food cultures of the west have existed on a route to our sleepy isle. Of particular importance to this book is the very last step before us, the *grande cuisine* of our friends across the channel. French cuisine is judged by UNESCO as so important to the human race it has been given the status of world intangible heritage. Hopefully some of the recipes included in coming pages will also go to show how French tradition itself was built upon those places earlier on the imaginary route. These places also possess incredible ideas in their kitchens, North Africa and the Middle East built the foundations of European food. Spices and people travelled along routes ending in France and knowledge travelled with them. Darwinian evolutionists should assume, with a pinch of salt, that the food furthest down the line would be most highly evolved to its niche. Britain is of course, the end of the line. As I personally do not believe the inhabitants of North America will pick up quite where we and France have left off.

It is fun to dream up pretend stories of just how fish and chips was invented but the purpose here is not to write a concise history of food. Despite this I include this introduction as I do believe it would be possible to exemplify subtle similarities and differences between the foods of geographically close locations on this map by looking at variations of dishes they produce. Recipes and menus link the globe together, on many levels. My hypothesis is the lines drawn below show how the foods we all have all are linked through a long history of human migration, trade and most importantly, people sharing meals together.

Research on the next steps for food logically begins at home, the present 'final-stage' of food evolution in this story. Yet, a man with eyes only for the future is blind in both, and thus we must look to our neighbours for advice. Although 'British' cuisine is already so influenced by the classic French ways there are always new things to think about. Britons accept food from all over the globe as their own, they study and develop it, partly why we eat such a globalised diet. I will propose taking what is now the 'British' and viewing it through a French lens. The framing is provided by our lovely house in Itzac which was home last year to four English students for a week.

Itzac is a farming village on a hill, a single steep road bordered with in the flowers of early summer. At the bottom of the hill there is a washhouse, a stone building perhaps 500 years old. In the middle of the town and halfway up of the hill there is an old school building, still in use. At the top, after a number of traditional rural French houses (all with beautiful gardens) the village ends, as smoothly as it began, all that is left is an incredible view. Although sparsely populated and always quiet, apart from two minutes at the end of the school day, Itzac has both grown and shrunk throughout the ages of 'culinary history' we have been speaking of here. It now possesses an immense population of one hundred and fifty-one (2015). Many of whom are foreign, English, and probably reside elsewhere a great deal of the time. Very little can be known about Itzac through written records, especially on the internet, the few Occitan speaking locals are probably the only ones to know what the village is really all about.

Map depicting the progression of great food cultures in Europe, North Africa and the Near East

The Mediterranean Diet.

Thankfully for the French, numerous cross-cultural data analysis studies show that Mediterranean countries have some of the lowest rates of cardiac health related illness (strokes and heart attacks) in the world. It is assumed by many researchers that the cause of this trend is largely dietary as within a nation many things may vary but diet, on a whole, stays fairly consistent through a population where other significant health predictors like exercise levels do not.

A comparative study by the Australian Institute of Health and Welfare found the only countries with lower rates of coronary heart disease than France, Spain, Greece and Italy (listed in order, lowest first) were Japan and Hong Kong. These statistics should be doubly impressive as Japan, Spain and Greece also have the highest rates of adult smokers worldwide. The Asian diet has long been appreciated for its healthiness, comprising largely of rice, fish and fermented vegetables, all of which are known to promote gut health and contain few saturated fats; but it is not quite the same as that of the Mediterraneans.

Indeed, the people of *la mer Méditerranée* also eat a lot of fish, something this book will promote, large amounts of which come straight out of the sea from which they also take their name. They cook with unrefined, fresh, olive oils and natural goose or pig fats. These reasonably 'good' fats are used alongside abundances of fresh fruits and vegetables, garden grown herbs and excellent recipes in which to use them all, which must be helpful. But in addition to this they consume the largest quantities of red wine in the world, besides the U.S.A, (which is clearly a far more populated nation). Clearly over-consumption is to be avoided but the Europeans, unlike many Brits, do drink in moderation. Another noted aspect of life in these temperate climbs is that eating together with family and friends and taking pleasure in one's food leads to a positive mental state and healthy attitudes to food and consumption itself. I for one vastly prefer sharing my cooking and eating with friends to dining alone, though sometimes it is nice to at least cook in peace.

I speculate that what we can learn from this is. Sunshine, fish, vegetables, quality olive oil, and appreciation for the occasional glass of quality wine may be a solution to a few of the problems that our own country faces. And furthermore, government sponsored distribution of this book may resolve the issue of an underfunded NHS.

Menu

Notes on the recipes.

- As stated above, all recipes are given to serve four unless specified, the quantities are easily adjusted,
- Pans should be heated until slightly smoking before anything, even oil, is added to them,
- Bread is brown unless a French *baguette*,
- Cooking times are never definite. All will depend on equipment and size of cut being used, use your senses and experience,
- Herbs are fresh from the garden except where otherwise stated,
- Buy organic or free-range ingredients when possible, these taste better, are better for you and support sustainable farming,
- Butter is salted,
- Chopping instructions are hard to give in words alone. You may have to re-read and improvise, or, use the internet to research the 'correct' ways to do some kitchen tasks. These save a lot of time.
- Salt, black pepper and olive oil for frying are not listed as ingredients unless specific quantities are required. Their presence in the kitchen and the majority of recipes is assumed,
- 'Salt' means sea-salt.

Assiettes.

Food is incredibly adaptable. Often, we consider different dishes to be more suitable as a starter or side rather than a main, yet this brittle thinking is unnecessary. Spanish cuisine accepts tapas as a norm, in Greece a similar concept is called meze; these very social ways of cooking and eating enable participants to sample wide varieties of dishes and share them with friends. in France will be focused on. In the heat, eating light and often is a good idea, this avoids the after dinner 'food coma' that is made all the worse by Mediterranean heat. For this, small assiettes (English: plates or dishes) are best.

I encourage readers to think about how the plates listed in this chapter and the next could be used in combination to create full table sized feasts or reduced and enlarged to suit specific times in a formal dinner. Thousands more plates and recipe elements could be included in this section but a select few from my time in France will be focused on.

Additional considerations often made at the start of a meal are carefully paired aperitifs. I will leave particulars of this decision to the discerning alcohol enthusiast. My personal recommendation however, for all cooks and diners, is a selection of wines throughout the meal. Whites and lighter reds should be poured at this time. Locally to Itzac, a large amount of impeccable rosé is produced and consumed. It is ideal for cooking on a hot day; lightweight, mildly fruity, and not over-sweetened. This wine was of the highest quality and outstrips all rose I have had before – especially cheaper varieties from British supermarkets. In this instance life in rural France cannot be replicated at home. Even with a sturdy culinary guide in hand.

Menu

Curried Mackerel Fillet with Radish and Tomato Tzatziki.

At the time of writing I consider this dish to be one of the finest things ever conceived by the human mind. It's time to end the contests for the freshest, lightest and most colourful summer plate ladies and gentlemen – there is a winner. The dish is made in two parts, both can be done in advance and kept in the fridge for several days, or prepared and served at a relaxed pace for an early supper in the garden. The marinated curry flavour mackerel deliberately avoids chilli to keep it refreshing; like coronation chicken it is spiced but not spicy. The addition of tomato and radish to a standard tzatziki adds substance and summer colours, it becomes like a Raita, a very versatile Indian dip. This dish is appropriate at any point in the meal - but I think most of it as a starter. Try to source food fresh and locally, especially fish, which should have shiny skin and bright sparkling eyes. Mackerel is remarkably safe and if sourced appropriately may even be eaten raw. Undercooking therefore does not present a huge threat if you follow appropriate hygiene practices in the kitchen but; trust your nose and don't waste time or money on unworthy produce.

Ingredients;

For the Mackerel;
Two Whole Mackerel or Four Fillets,
2 Tbsp. Turmeric,
1 Tbsp. Soy Sauce,
1 Tbsp. Lemon Juice,
½ Tbsp. Cumin,
3 Garlic Cloves,
Thumb of Ginger.

For the Tzatziki:
400g Full Fat Greek Yoghurt,
1/3 Cucumber,
4 Salad Tomatoes,
8 Large Radishes,
Handful of Mint (and some leaf pairs for decoration),
2 Tbsp Lemon Juice.

Method;

Here we are making a marinade for the fish and then leaving it to relax in the fridge for several hours, it is therefore sensible to start on this before creating the salad. Combine all dry ingredients in a bowl with a dash of olive oil so that a loose paste is formed, season with salt and pepper. Peel the ginger with the back of a spoon, crush this and the garlic using a hand tool or knife, add to the marinade. Depending the source of you fresh fish the mackerel may or may not need to be filleted. Do this with care following online instructions; it is a skill to be learnt, not easily taught on one page. Place the four fillets in a dish and pour over the curry marinade, it should make contact with all the flesh. Flip the fillets over several times to ensure the coating is thorough. Cover with cling film, or to avoid waste a lid, and place in the fridge and leave for several hours. When it is time to serve, the fillets should be cooked ideally on a griddle, skin down, until almost done and then briefly flipped onto their tops to cook through. They may also be done on a barbeque or in an oven on the grill setting. The fish is cooked when beginning to flake apart.

For the tzatziki the cucumber should be halved lengthways, and the wet centre removed with the back of a teaspoon. The lengths are then to be cut across-ways, creating very thin half-moon shapes. This is done with varying speed and accuracy depending on your knife skills; accuracy is overrated, and oddly sized chunks may be excused as artistic flare. To prepare the tomatoes, cut into quarters and deseed each at a time by running the knife from the bottom up, underneath the wet core and flat on top of the substantial outer skin. These deseeded tomato quarters should then be sliced into long, thin sections. Structural integrity of the radish discs must be maintained while making them as thin as is reasonable to maximise their aesthetic qualities. Wash them, remove both ends and carefully cut into discs. The mint leaves must also be chopped, finely, but not into a dust. Only one pass of the knife should be made as excessive chopping will release the oils that contain the mint flavour onto the surface and not into the salad. All ingredients are combined in the yoghurt with salt and then mixed, gently.

Potato and Rocket *Gratin Dauphinois*.

Gratin *dauphinois* is truly French, it hails from the south eastern region that goes by the same name, but now known worldwide. A good *gratin* makes accompaniment to myriad dishes and may also be consumed chilled. Although this may not seem the most interesting recipe, and certainly it cannot form a meal in itself, ignoring it from this book would be an act of war of French cuisine. A culinary arms race that can never be won. Potato choice is of high importance and I side with those who suggest using waxier yellow spuds that will hold their own when cooked. This usually results in a desirably firm, presentable stack for the plate. The challenge to tradition here is to make the *Gratin* on the hob in a deep skillet pan, however, the same ingredients can be baked for a classic *dauphinois* and there is little difference in the result. Sun-dried tomatoes are a possible addition, with the rocket, but if they are used excess oil should be dabbed off on a kitchen towel.

Ingredients;
500g Potatoes (Waxy is best),
200ml Double Cream,
50g Cheddar Cheese,
150g Rocket,
4 Garlic Cloves,
1 Tbsp. *Herbs de Provence (*dried is acceptable here, the usual jars contain large variety of common herbs so if only fresh varieties are available substitute for the maximum number of these, finely chopped).

Method;

Rinse and slice the potatoes into many thin slices (around 5mm thick). The safest and fastest way to do this is to take one slice off the largest face of the spud and discard it. This gives the potato a flat side that it can comfortably sit on while being chopped. If it cannot roll around fingers are kept on hands. In the large pan slightly fry off the garlic, the cloves left whole but crushed. Add the potatoes, a splash of water and herbs, allow to cook until some take a on little colour. They will not need to cook the whole way through but may start to crumble at the edges, for this reason, all stirring should be gentle. Add to the pan at this point the cream and three quarters of the rocket. Carefully encourage these ingredients between all possible overlaps of potato and season with salt. After this point no more stirring or agitation should be done, the potatoes will absorb some of the liquid and begin to cook into each-other, hopefully forming a firm tower. Turn down the heat to a very low simmer after the cream begins to bubble for the first time as overheating will burn it to the pan. When a knife can pass through all the potatoes and the liquid is reduced somewhat finish off by topping with cheddar cheese and grilling for several minutes. If confident in the solidity of your gratin: flip and drop it with gusto onto a chopping board where it can be sliced. Remaining rocket is to go on top afterwards, it will sink in slightly and become 'attached' to the gratin.

Baguette Tradition.

The people of France have a relationship with bread unlike us. The baguette can do many things. It may sit on the side of any table at any mealtime. A *baguette tradition,* easily enough translated, is the original staple food. It is protected by a 1993 law and must be made in house, by hand and use only four ingredients, flour, water, salt and yeast. The *tradition* is inherently variable, each *boulangerie* has its own style, because each is made by a different hand. This is a perfect excuse for the imperfections of home baking. Bread can be made each morning, for the day, it is simple enough, and anyone descending the stairs in the morning who catches a whiff of warming yeast will smile; even if they are gluten intolerant and may never taste the product. The mix needs to rest at several points in the recipe, find somewhere warm for this like a windowsill or tepid radiator.

Ingredients;

400g Flour (300g plain white and 100g of bread flour is best but all plain is fine),
300ml Water (Warm or part boiled, too hot and it will kill the yeast),
7g Yeast (Either dry active yeast or bakers yeast is fine),
1tsp. Sugar.

Method;

Place the yeast, sugar and warm water in a jug. Cover with a damp tea-towel and, for the first of several times, leave to rest in a warm place (30 minutes). In a bowl slowly incorporate the yeast mix into all of the flour with a large pinch of salt to create wet mixture, cover with a damp tea-towel and leave to rest in a warm place (1 hour).

Drop the dough mixture onto a floured surface and divide into four equal parts; continue to apply dustings of flour until the dough is workable on the surface. Kneading is not necessary but gently encourage the dough pieces to become flat rectangles and fold them over onto themselves once or twice like an envelope. Cover with a damp tea-towel and leave to rest in a warm place (1 hour).

By hand, shape into four balls of dough into long thin batons. The dough should be slightly elastic, smell yeasty, and have a smooth surface. To hold the batons in shape, and prevent them touching, place another tea-towel inside the tray and pinch ridges into it to fit the batons. Cover with a damp tea-towel, and, leave to rest in a warm place (1 hour).

Before the hour is up preheat the oven and a tray to 180*c. When hot, flour the tray and place the batons on it. Score the tops of them diagonally and place in the oven for 25 minutes. Remove when crisp and golden brown. Allow to cool before slicing.

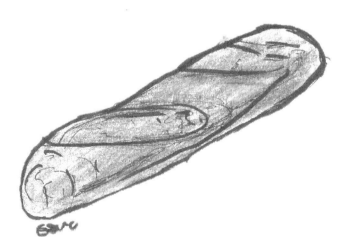

Spicy Trout Ceviche.

Although it is not French or British this painfully simple South American dish is an excellent one to share with friends in the sun and therefore makes it to our table in France. It may be served on one large platter or individual plates; either way can look delightfully colourful with minimal decoration. This particular recipe comes out rather hot. Yet, balanced with other flavours and in small doses, even chilli-phobic individuals prove able to enjoy it as an appetiser. Adapting to a larger fruit and avocado based salad is a viable opportunity to convert this small dish into a main course.

Ingredients;

1 Whole Rainbow Trout or Two Fillets,

 (Almost any other fish variety is suitable, in reality, little of the original flavour will be maintained but the colour of the trout is nice, Bass, Bream and Haddock are good alternatives),

Juice of 2 Lemons,

(This is the only ingredient besides the fish that may never be omitted, improvisation elsewhere is encouraged),

2-3 Whole Hot Red Chillies,

½ Red Onion,

Small Handful Coriander,

Fingertip of Ginger,

Colourful Salad Items to Decorate.

Method;

In a mixing bowl combine the zest of one lemon and the juice of two; add the chillies, coriander and ginger, finely chopped, and the red onion diced into small cubes. Add oil, salt and pepper, and stir. The trout should then be retrieved and placed on a chopping board. If it is whole the fish must first be filleted (audio-visual aids are a help here). Although care should be taken to remove all sizeable bones I have found that after cutting and 'cooking' the fish none of the very small ones that were left in could be found in the final product; this is a relief as bone removal can be a painstaking process.

When filleted the next step is to create thin slices of fish. Holding the thicker end of the fillet cut at the tail end first (away from the securing hand), gentle cuts are made at a 45* angle (to increase surface area of each slice). When the knife slices through all the flesh turn it flat to the board removing the flesh from the skin, which is to be discarded, with practice the process becomes very simple but it can be difficult at first to get a good feeling for the fish.

If intending to serve the Ceviche on a large sharing board, lay out the individual slices on the tray as close together as is possible and cover thoroughly with the prepared juice. When serving on individual plates it is most efficient to put all the slices into the mixing bowl that contains the juices, stir and ensure all fish is under the surface. The fish is 'cooked' by citrus acids changing its protein structures – colour change from raw pink to white indicates this happening. Preference for texture dictates at what point one desires to serve the ceviche but leaving it for less than ten minutes is not recommended before this point it will remain fairly raw.

Fig Preserve.

This collection would not earn its title without a smattering of fig related recipes. Although fig trees grow no longer in the garden of Les Figues their fruits are still available from the local supermarket, even before their season, which is useful when we do not have three years to spare waiting to propagate a crop of our own. Although I do not appreciate the taste nor texture of a fig their delicate beauty and deep history allures me. The fig was reportedly one of the first cultivated plant species. We know this from fossil evidence and also from the fact Adam and Eve, the first humans, used fig leaves to cover their genitals in the garden of Eden. A good chutney goes with anything; this slightly sweet preserve works with cheese, or alone, on toast in the morning.

Ingredients;
6 Fresh Figs,
1 Large White Onion,
½ Cooking Apple,
100ml Cider Vinegar,
100g Brown Sugar,
2 Handfuls Sultanas,
2 Cloves.

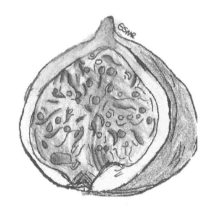

Method;
Chop the figs, onion and apple into small chunks of similar sizes. Regular shapes will look best in the final product. Combine all ingredients on a low heat and simmer for around an hour, stirring regularly, until the mix becomes very thick and sticky. Decant and store in a sterilised jar; it will keep for years if only entered with clean implements.

Breakfast Baked Eggs.

A past journey to the nation of Tunisia, which was a French colony until 1956, showed me one egg dish that solves one of Britain's largest problems. That of the boring breakfast. This revolutionary new knowledge was however left neglected for over a year. Until one morning in Southern France when, in an attempt to continue a streak of excellent meals, from the bag it was finally pulled. Although for some this may already seem obvious research was done revealing the secrets of *Shakshuka*. Pulled slightly further in line with the colonial regime's cuisine, and the contents of our fridge, this now tested recipe has been created. The Tunisian way was to have the vegetables cut chunky, which has influenced other pages of this book, but is not included here. This is mainly for ease of eating and to facilitate each portion, ideally, being made and served in its own small pan. Any meat cut to reasonable size, or none, may be used. But ensure the salty smouldering chilli flavours of good chorizo meat are replaced by other means early on if it is removed. The 'serving suggestion' here is good bread; fried in rosemary oil and indeed also chopped rosemary. Toast would also be sufficient.

Ingredients (serves one);

1 Egg,

½ A Green Pepper,

3cm Chorizo

¼ A White Onion,

¼ Tin Chopped Tomatoes (Un-chopped tomatoes can always be chopped),

¼ Garlic Bulb,

1 tsp. Oregano,

½ tsp. Paprika (More if the chorizo is omitted),

½ tsp. Chilli Flakes,

Sprigs of Rosemary and Thyme,

Handful of Grated Cheddar Cheese,

Rosemary fried bread to serve.

Method;

For the Shakshuka;

Chop the green pepper, onion and garlic into small lengths and set aside (retain one clove of garlic). Make small 1 cm squared cubes of chorizo by slicing the sausage into strips and then cutting across. Fry the chorizo briefly in a pan of salted oil then add the vegetables while stirring or tossing (the pan should ideally be small and have a lid). Add the seasonings at this point. Stir. When the vegetables are softened add chopped tomatoes from the tin and stir so that the tomatoes do not just sit on top. Lower the temperature to a simmer and reduce the liquid slightly. Drop the egg into a small hole in the tomato pan, make this using the back of a spoon. Lay grated cheese over the top and put the lid on the pan to increase the heat. The egg will take about five minutes to cook to the point of having a runny core, after which the dish is ready to eat.

For the Rosemary Fried Bread;

Heat a large flat frying pan for the bread just before the eggs are added to the shakshuka. Finely chop all the rosemary and crack the garlic clove, add these to the pan with a generous few tablespoons of oil and the desired quantity of bread slices. Fry at high heat on both sides until golden and crispy. Serve sliced alongside the egg which may be left in its original pan or decanted on top of the toast.

Baked Rice with Pomegranate and Olive.

Rice is a humble foodstuff that has deservedly earned god like respect in some kitchens of the east; to western chefs it often presents itself as a problem, I know many, and many struggle. Baking rice is an unusual method to circumventing the usual difficulties. It works simply by hiding them behind the oven door. Occasionally a peek can be snuck but eventually all glory is revealed when the dish is removed from the oven - exactly like Christmas morning. The rice, if perfectly cooked, will retain infinite separation and fluffiness below a slightly crisped surface. It looks appealing and is ready to serve straight from the oven alongside a variety of other dishes. Debate often arises over rinsing rice, when boiling I am a strong advocate, yet in dishes where the rice cooks slower it seems to have less impact on the outcome. A brief rinse may be necessary to remove dust from particularly 'authentic' brands.

Ingredients;

250g White Rice,	1 Lemon,
Seeds of Half a Pomegranate,	
250g Pitted Green Olives (Or mixed),	Full Fat Greek Yoghurt and a
½ Red Onion,	small handful of Parsley to serve.

Method;

De-seed the pomegranate by slicing in half and prising apart the flesh from the pips, place these in a bowl. Cut the olives crossways in order to create several small rounds from each and dice onion into small cubes. Half the lemon should be retained for juice and the other half cut into several rounds. All of these should also be put aside for now. Preheat the oven (fan at 200*c). Slightly oil the base of a presentable oven dish and add the rice. My usual practice is to use half of the chopped ingredients during cooking and half on top; these are added, and all is mixed. Include at this point a generous pinch of salt and squeeze of lemon juice. Cover the rice in water that is almost twice its depth, put it in the hot place, and wait pensively. Putting a lid on the dish or covering it with tin foil will change the nature of the grains at the end of the process - there seems to be no harm in leaving it uncovered. This in fact makes it easier to periodically make visual checks on the dish. If all the water disappears before the rice is fully cooked do not worry, liquid will remain out of sight and cooking will continue. Remove the rice when the top layer starts to become slightly crisp. At this point it can either be fluffed with a fork, as one would usually do with boiled rice, or left with a crunchy outer layer, I choose the latter. Top the rice with the rings of lemon, remaining Olives and pomegranate and some small dollops of yoghurt. Rough chopped parsley and cracked black pepper are the final finish.

Toasted Peri-Peri Chickpeas.

A simple snack and also a good way of emptying the back of a cupboard when moving out of a house. Chickpeas are multifunctional and may equally well be made into hummus. But when there are no crisps, they must be both chip and dip.

Ingredients;
1 Tin of Chickpeas,
1 Tbsp. Paprika,
2 tsp. Chilli Powder,
2 tsp. Salt.

Method;
Preheat the oven to 200*c. Peel and rinse the chickpeas then cover them with the seasonings listed by tossing in a large bowl. Roast until crispy.

Grilled Peach with Mozzarella and Serrano Ham.

A gently balanced salad of summer flavours that also looks great on a plate; the dish can be easily adapted into a main by the addition of some leaves and roasted vegetables. This triumvirate of flavours has been rumoured to steal the hearts of men and women alike; it should be deployed with care and only used on special occasions - like birthdays. Although the peach should only really appear in late summer it is usually available all year round in both the UK and France thanks to the powers of agro-business. Mildly under-ripened peaches are actually ideal this one as they stay firm under heat. Either way, grilling greatly enhances the flavour of the peaches as it re-structures the sugars they contain. Very little instruction is required here beyond the title but it will, of course, be offered. Note also that figs, or *figues* as they are now known, would make an excellent salad in place of the peach. They are prepared in the same way but may require a mildly acidic dressing to tease out their taste.

Ingredients;
3 Peaches,
2 Balls of Mozzarella (This is slightly too much, to allow for some to be eaten while cooking),
4 Slices of Serrano Ham,
6 Tbsp. Running Honey,
Mint to Garnish.

Method;
Heat Grill to 200*c, It is important to add the peaches to an already hot environment as slowly increasing their temperature causes sogginess. On a baking tray place the peaches, halved through the centre, stones removed if possible (if doing this threatens the structure of the peach leave them in as after cooking it will be much easier). Sprinkle a pinch of rock salt on to each half then cover with honey. Place under the grill; preparation is done as all other work will be done on the plate. Keep an eye on the peaches, cooking time will vary depending on ripeness, but we are aiming for a darkening colour and softness throughout. When they are grilled remove and allow to cool (they may be served lukewarm but not hot). A beautiful golden pink liquid will be expelled from the fruit, if in quantity, it may be collected and used to decorate the plates. With my serving suggestion four entire halves should be kept and the remaining two cut into halves, the mozzarella and ham should be torn not cut and an arrangement of all these elements made on the plate. If juice was collected this, and the mint leaves, may be used for further decoration.

Cod *Feuilles De Brick* with Homemade Mayonnaise.

Moroccan cuisine without the cumin. These parcels may be served sliced as a starter or full size with leaves and a beer for a summer lunch. This is an easy one to make but the love that goes into making your own mayonnaise rather than buying it usually earns respect at the table – it will also taste better. The concept of a filo roll is strong, this recipe itself is just one incarnation of an idea, it may be changed to accommodate vegetarians, or imitate specific regional dishes. Gluten free filo pastry is available but I cannot speak for its quality as a substitute. Different chefs will have varying opinions on how mayonnaise is to be made, depending on their training and level of pedanticality[1]. Though creating it by hand is a magical experience where one gets to slowly create a sauce far larger in volume than the sum of the component parts, in a strange kind of gastronomic alchemy, it is perfectly reasonable and much more efficient - to use a blender.

Ingredients

For the Bricks;

Filo Pastry Roll,
450g Cod (Or Other White Fish),
300g Mixed Olives,
½ Bulb of Garlic,
150g Sundried Tomatoes,
100g Capers,
Small Handful Parsley,
1 tsp. Chilli Powder.

For Mayonnaise;

2 Egg Yolks,
100ml Rapeseed oil
2 tsp. Dijon Mustard
1 tsp. White Wine Vinegar,
1 tsp. Paprika Powder,
Small Handful Parsley,
Ice Cold Water as Required.

---

[1] Pedanticality – a pedantic individual's level of pedanticness. (neither of these are real words).

Method;

For the Mayonnaise;
Combine all the given ingredients (excluding the parsley and oil for now, to avoid unbound green sauce) in a blender, or if using a hand blender, in a bowl. Blend thoroughly. When the egg is creamed add 1/3 of the oil and blend again, the mixture should thicken slightly. Once again stop and add more oil. Should the sauce become too thick add more water to thin it out, adding oil will have the opposite effect and thus should be used to thicken a thin mayonnaise. When all of the oil is incorporated, and the desired texture reached, taste and season appropriately. Add the parsley, finely chopped, and stir through.

For the Bricks;
Preheat oven to 200*c. Prepare a chunky olive tapenade by repeatedly passing through the olives, capers, sundried tomatoes and parsley. Make the garlic into a fine paste by covering it in a large amount of salt before chopping, use the side of the knife to crush, a chemical reaction with salt will help break down the garlic into a paste. Mix this paste with the chopped ingredients in a bowl and stir while adding olive oil. Season with salt, pepper and chilli (the chilli is not enough to make the dish spicy but just broadens the base of flavours). On an oiled or floured surface lay one sheet of the pastry, paint its upper surface in oil and lay a second sheet, at an angle, over the top. Identify how the longest parcel may be created. When this is decided lay an even line of fish, to achieve evenness the fish may need to be divided into smaller parts, top with less tapenade in a ratio of 2:1. The parcels do not need to be overfilled and should fold up easily from each side and the ends, to the size of a large sausage roll. Trim off excess pastry, score the top and baste with more oil. Repeat the process with the rest of the fish and pastry. Cook for around 20 minutes or until the pastry starts to turn golden. Each brick may or may not need to be sliced, this depends on how big they have been made and what purpose they have in the meal. Trimming off the very ends to reveal the cross-sectional view is recommended in all cases; this also offers an opportunity to be certain the fish is cooked through.

Pea Soup.

Having never made pea soup before stepping into this beautiful French kitchen it was surprising to see how well this improvised recipe, which was essentially an attempt to clear up leftover ingredients, turned out. Veteran and virgin pea soup eaters around the garden table were all pleased – which made me doubly pleased. The soup is a perfect illustration of my argument for improvisation and substitution. This is indeed probably why soups and stews have been so popular over the history of human cooking. Basic elements: salt, fat, acid (and heat), if you wish to quote Samin Nosrat's lovely book, can be sourced from a multitude of ingredients but only need to be balanced appropriately to create a fine meal. With this optimistic outlook comes a warning; not everything tastes good in combination. But, its usually worth trying. When working on a soup one may even take a spoonful of soup and try it with a small amount of the ingredient that is under consideration. Much like an artist tests colours on his palette before applying them to the canvass. I believe the key piece of the puzzle here is good fat, used here is a rind of dried meat and cheese. This base is not as nutritionally 'good' as using quality bone stocks, but it certainly holds more flavour.

Ingredients;

500g Frozen Peas,
1 Medium Potato,
½ White Onion,
2 Garlic Cloves,
75g Butter,
50g of Fatty edges from any Cured Ham
or Bacon,

50g Blue Cheese,
Handful of Mint,
1 Tbsp. Vegetable Bullion or Stock,
Pepper and Salt (weren' t expecting
that were you),

Plain Yoghurt to Serve.

Method;

For this recipe it is best, though not essential, to finely dice the potato and onion as cooking is quicker when there are no large chunks. Locate a suitably sized saucepan and heat it up. With butter salt and a splash of water brown the onion and cook the potato cubes; this is best done with the lid on to maintain moisture. There is no chance of overcooking this recipe but stir attentively enough to not ruin the pan. Add chopped garlic, meat fat and bullion powder in with the peas allow these to cook for a while before including the mint (stems removed) and cheese. The recipe lists pepper and salt in this un-aesthetic order to highlight the absurd quantities of black pepper that should be included, the pepper mill should be turned so much it becomes dizzy. Reduce the heat and allow to simmer for a while. When confident remove from the heat and allow to cool for several minutes before blending. Aim for a very smooth texture but do not pulse or rearrange the contents of the blender too much - simply blend until the majority is good. The purpose of this negligence is to leave several unbroken peas to populate the dish, this is a nice touch. When intending to serve; reheat the soup and decorate with yoghurt, pepper and a mint leaf.

Chicken Liver Pate.

Pate makes an excellent snacking material or starter - it is much loved. While all other recipes in this book are given for feeding four people making such a small amount of pate would be impractical. Additionally, it is so moreish that many more than one serving is usually taken. A pate can be kept in the fridge and may be eaten at breakfast, lunch and dinner. Though this is not very healthy as pate is simply a meat flavoured butter. This recipe contains lashings of port and brandy, it is a commonly held belief that cooking removes the alcohol from a food. However, this is not completely true, especially in low heat cooking, unless for many hours. When you *flambé* the contents of the pan in this recipe a significant amount of alcohol will burn off, but probably not all, so don't feed grandma too much pate. Making this dish is especially messy unless it is executed with immense levels of care so it is recommended to wear your finest Sunday clothes.

Ingredients;

400g Chicken Livers,

400g Butter,

300ml Port,

300ml Brandy (both measures of alcohol are a rough guide, use plenty),

5 Shallots,

1 Garlic Bulb,

Several Rosemary Sprigs,

Several Thyme Sprigs,

1 Tbsp. Salt (One 'chefs pinch').

Method;

Collect all ingredients in bowls as the process is time dependant and having everything close at hand increases speed. Find a desirable pate dish, which will need to be sizeable, and line it with cling film. The shallots and garlic should be finely diced, butter softened and the herbs with their stems removed - chopped. One bowl may be prepared containing the herbs, garlic, salt and some pepper, mixed. Heat a large pan with some of the butter, when this is melted and the pan hot add some shallots when they begin to soften add some of the livers with herbs, garlic and salt. It is not necessary to do them all at once and there should be ample room for movement in the pan. The livers should be cooked to only 62.5*c, overcooking will harm the outcome as they become tough, keep checking with the temperature probe while flicking or stirring to ensure even heat distribution. As the temperature rises into the 50's*c prepare to add several glugs of port, followed with brandy. Use the kitchen lighter to ignite the alcohol and watch as large flames rise. The correct temperature has probably been reached, check, and if correct remove from the heat.

Combine the pan contents with a roughly equal weight of butter in a blender. Pulse until smooth. It is a matter of preference but usually I favour leaving some texture. While it is still hot pour the mixture into the lined tray. Repeat the process until all the livers and butter are exhausted. The surface of what is now a liquid pate in the tray should be smoothed and a layer of cling film put over it. Refrigerate for several hours to solidify. When serving the cling film should allow the pate to be easily put onto a chopping board, leaving it wrapped up use a hot knife to slice portions, remember to remove the cling film from the slice. Serve with toast, a small dressed salad and possibly a chutney.

Sautéed Potatoes.

I often create a variation of this dish when struggling with the fact that the only foods in the house are spices – which are frankly no good on their own. These potatoes can be developed into a great side or snack; no garden feast will ever really be complete without them. As with the gratin above fairly waxy potatoes are best. It is important the wedges can handle the abuse they are given in the pan while being able to absorb some fats. Equally essential is the skill of not boiling over-par in the first place, as the potatoes will be cooked some more in the frying pan. The point here may seem obvious but if one does not think ahead while cooking about how different processes will interact then the result will rarely be as good as it could be. When logical considerations like this are made in the kitchen anything is achievable by even the modestly experienced cook. Chilli levels are a matter of preference but sometimes pushing the boundaries is a good idea; in combination with other foods what may seem volcanic on its own can become quite pleasant.

Ingredients;

700g Potatoes,
100ml Pasata,
50g Chorizo,
50g Butter
½ White Onion,
4 Garlic Cloves,

2 Tbsp. Tomato Puree,
2 tsp. Smoked Paprika,
2 tsp. Chilli Flakes (or a crushed dried chilli),
Several Basil Leaves,

Sour Cream to Serve.

Method;

Slice the potatoes into the size of your dream wedge, small enough to easily fit in the mouth. Try to avoid creating actual wedges. The precipice of the triangle is thin and will overcook and break too easily. Par boil the chunks in salted water – this is until a knife can easily cut most of the way through. Drain and leave to stand with the lid removed. In a large frying pan or wok fry the onion, which should be diced and the chorizo, cubed. This should be done at high heat, crispiness not softness is desired. Add the potatoes and the other seasonings when the onion is browned and stir to evenly fry. Continue to add more as it is absorbed or fried off. In the same way slowly add the passata, if it is all incorporated to soon there will be moisture causing the potatoes to steam/boil not fry. Some edges may break off but if the heat is adequate, they will seal themselves back up and become crispy. Be liberal with the salt and pepper and serve when crispy and dark, drenched in puddles of sour cream.

Garlic and Rosemary Olives.

I include this as a side note, a proof, a salvation, both that any flavour can be harnessed at home and, that supermarket olives are overpriced. Most mornings in France I was reminded sternly that we would shortly need to prepare the days olives to avoid disappointment in mid-afternoon sun. Anyone with a favourite flavour of olive deserves the satisfaction of creating that taste for themselves. Only by seasoning and leaving the olives for several hours (longer is of course better) any plain green or black jar olive can be reborn as an aromatic, pungent and decadent taste-ball. Garlic and rosemary are my go to notes and were also the most abundant ingredients at the time. Adding some extra olive oil is recommended but the olives do not need to be submerged. It is easiest just to retain most of their original brine.

Ingredients;

300g Plain Green Olives (Being plain is not essential but will simplify matters),
4 Garlic Cloves,
Several Rosemary Sprigs.

Method;

Remove some of the brine from the olive jar. Finely chop both the garlic and rosemary without turning them into a complete dust. Combine these with 1 Tbsp. of salt and olive oil in the jar or a bowl (too much oil will go solid in the fridge). Shake or stir to make sure the seasonings make their rounds - for extra effects try manually stuffing the pit holes with garlic. Leave for several hours or a day in the fridge - when serving drizzle with olive oil to restore the freshest possible look to the olives.

Asparagus Shoots with Hollandaise.

Legend has it that beautiful green asparagus shoots go out of season as soon as the final weekend of Ascot starts. This not only means nothing to the French but is also clearly nonsense as the timing of a horse race has very little bearing on the weather conditions in early summer. The frightful tale of hollandaise sauce, however, is true, and can make many a chef tremble in fear like an actor in the Scottish play at only the mention of its name. Especially if he is in a rush. This dish is absurdly simple but delicious; it is unknown (and irrelevant) whether it is a starter or a breakfast.

Ingredients;

20 Small Green Asparagus (five each),   1 Tbsp. Lemon juice
400g Butter,   1 tsp. White Pepper,
4 Egg Yolks,   Water as Required,
2 Tbsp. White Wine Vinegar,   Tomatoes to Serve.

Method;

Prepare the asparagus by peeling, with a peeler, away the tougher outer skin which is usually found around the base. To make perfect spears lay them down and trim all to the same length; this will vary depending on the growth of the asparagus at hand. To cook prepare a large pan of boiling water and blanche the spears in the water for 1-2 minutes; it is important to retain some bite. Remove from the pan and immediately refresh in ice cold water. When they are thoroughly cooled pat dry and store in the fridge.

To make a hollandaise sauce; in a saucepan slowly melt the butter until it starts to clarify – do not let it burn. Simultaneously reduce the vinegar, with 1 tbsp. of water and the white pepper, by more than half by boiling rapidly – allow the reduction to cool by removing it from the pan. In a third and final saucepan the sauce will be made. Cautious cooks will simmer water in the pan and secure a heat safe bowl above it to form a Bain Marie. However, I favour working straight in the pan as temperature may be controlled more easily by removing it from the heat. This control is so important with making hollandaise as a very low cooking temperature must be maintained to prevent scrambling of the egg yolks. Over minimal heat gently whisk the egg yolks with vinegar reduction until a sabayon is formed. This is when the texture is thick enough to show impressions of the whisk on its surface. Should evidence of scrambling appear, usually by streaks of egg forming, instantly remove from the heat and try to recover with a small amount of water. If the effects are severe, start again, you will now better understand the temperature desired and will be able to maintain it by manually adjusting the pans proximity to the heat. When the sabayon is formed slowly incorporate the butter while continuing to gently whisk. If the sauce becomes too stiff add a small amount of water or lemon juice. When the correct texture is reached, enough to lightly coat a spoon, season to taste with lemon juice. Store the sauce at a warm room temperature. When serving arrange the asparagus spears as desired, pour over the hollandaise and place under the grill until golden. Decorate with finely chopped cubes of tomato. Hollandaise contains semi-raw egg and should be eaten with caution by those who are vulnerable. It should be discarded at the end of the day.

Oeufs en Meurette.

When finding this for the first time in Elizabeth David's 1950 classic work, *A Book of Mediterranean Food*, it struck me as unusual. Since then it has become apparent not only that poaching eggs in red wine should be considered normal because it is so delicious but also that, in France, it is normal. The recipe given here is a simpler than some; but it is a good place to start. Not everyone will make eggs-*au-vin* part of their daily routine but everyone should try it. Away from home, on a scorching hot French morning the difference in temperature between the egg (which is removed from the heat a while before serving) and the still warm sauce will be negligible. I have often found it difficult to eat in these temperatures and often break my fast indoors for safety. There is half a bottle of red wine left over from the night before but this is confusing as everyone has a bold hangover. Will cooking our eggs in alcohol be a haute-cuisine hair of the dog?

Ingredients

½ Bottle of Red Wine,
4 Eggs,
½ White Onion,
2 Garlic Cloves,
1 tsp. White Sugar (if the wine is not a sweet one),

Sprigs of Rosemary and Thyme with Other Stemmed Herbs for a *Bouquet Garni*,
Fried Bread to Serve.

Method;

In a large saucepan fry diced onion and garlic briefly before adding the wine, *bouquet garni*, sugar and some salt and pepper. Ensure the mixture reaches a boil and after several minutes remove the *bouquet* and poach the eggs. The correct way to do this is to whisk the saucepans contents in the same circular motion until a vortex forms in the middle. While it is still strong, crack the eggs into the centre. If the shells are broken with care the egg membranes will remain intact resulting in perfect poached eggs. This process is not specific to poaching in red wine but if water is used a small amount of vinegar should be added. Egg yolk liquidity is a matter of personal taste and only a few minutes is required to create the ideal poached egg. Remove the now purple eggs with a slotted spoon and place in a bowl lined with kitchen roll. Boil the contents hard to reduce them into a thicker sauce. A small amount of butter and flour might be used to speed up the process. Serve the poached eggs on top of herby fried bread with a significant helping of wine sauce.

Pernod *Flambé* King Prawns.

It seems no matter how this dish is presented it will always be somewhat reminiscent of a culture of eating obsessed with cheddar and pineapple skewers and the odd devilled egg – things that are not cool anymore. The mild kitschiness speaks to an age when 'fine' foods were finally reaching into the dinner parties of the middle class. I believe this is something we are experiencing again in this era when stay at home parents have access to obscure ingredients and recipes by top chefs on their phones. Even more important is recognising that these dinner party dishes were a way to show off one's decadence to friends. Today this can be done at breakfast - via Instagram. Bread is essential with this dish to mop up the delicious sauce that will fall into the bowl. Consider using a knob, these portion sized loaves are perfect and very easy to make.

Ingredients;

16 King Prawns (They must be raw, go for peeled prawns as this fiddly process is best done by a machine),
100ml Pernod (Aniseed liquor).
Large Handful of Tarragon

Handful of Parsley,
½ White Onion,
1 Large Mild Chilli,
1 Tbsp. Lemon Juice.

Method;

Dice the onion as finely as possible. Cut along one side of the chilli and remove the seeds and pith and then slice across on the bias (at a 45* angle) to create some beautiful long sections.

Heat a very large frying pan to full heat and fry off the onion in oil until soft but not brown. *Ensuite*, add the prawns, half the parsley, the tarragon, chilli slices, lemon juice and a pinch of salt and fry while continually flicking the pan. When the prawns begin to colour the Pernod should be added, it may ignite but if not will require a little encouragement from a blowtorch. Confident chefs will be able to light the alcohol while pouring it into the pan by catching a falling drop on an open flame or they will toss the pan through the flame to allow liquid and fire to meet. If this seems like a fire hazard use a kitchen lighter as was done in the pate recipe. The alcohol will burn with a high heat and finish them off, resulting in a crisp outer layer but not an overcooked prawn. Share the prawns and cooking liquid between small salad bottomed bowls. Garnish with the remaining parsley.

Camberzola and Fig Tray Bake.

Lost and ill-defined the Camberzola and fig tray bake cannot decide if it is a shared entree or sweetened after dinner cheeseboard. For arguments sake it will reside on this page. As a cheeseboard certainly this dish fills a need; it bridges the gap between sweet and savoury which such athletic skill nobody will know from which side it came. This is simply a combination of ingredients baked to bring out the richness of their flavours and served as a whole. This way anything, within reason, may be added and diners need only pick at what takes their fancy. For me the figs will be avoided, though one or two may slip though the net, disguised in dripping cheese.

Ingredients;

6 Figs (More if you have a fruitful tree),
1 Round Camberzola Cheese (Camembert is OK if you are blue phobic),
2 Rashers of Thin Cut Bacon,
50ml Running Honey,
1 Handful of Walnuts,
Sprigs of Rosemary and Thyme,

Baguette Tradition to Serve (Page. 18).

Method;

Preheat the oven to 200*c. In a large baking dish place all the ingredients. The cheese, at the centre, should be removed from any packaging. The figs can be halved or quartered depending on their size. The bacon should be sliced while uncooked using scissors into two cm wide sections along each rashers length. The figs, walnuts, bacon and herbs should be arranged on the tray around the cheese, so that they touch, overlap and hold each-other up off the base of the tray. Squeeze or drizzle honey over the top generously and apply several pinches of salt. Bake until the cheese is just starting to crack open or the bacon crispy. Serve with warm bread. If the baking tray is to be used on the table beware - it will be hot.

Buckwheat and Pickled Sultana Salad.

Despite being clearly labelled a wheat, buckwheat is gluten free. It is for this reason it is chosen over tabbouleh - which is also a very good grain. Making this salad is another excellent opportunity to fight back against the mint which by early summer begins to dominate the garden. Pickling sultanas requires several days of preparation ahead of time; the rest of the work can however be done very quickly and the result is a colourful and delicious salad. A multitude of additional salad items may be added these are simply the ones I recommend. It may not seem to be much, but this is a substantial meal, it seems to stand well enough on its own but is great with many other dishes, especially those from the BBQ. The art of pickling is a beautiful one, practiced by grandmothers and Eastern Europeans around the world. Mastery of this skill is important for those who wish to excel in the kitchen at home or commercially. I have found the need for only two types of pickling liquid no matter what ingredient is intended for the jar; one is plain, one is slightly spicy (and will not be used here). If good hygiene practices are followed one batch of liquid can support several rounds of pickling; with spicy pickles especially, the flavours will develop and become more potent over time.

Ingredients;

For the salad;

350g Buckwheat,
10 Medium Radishes,
4 Vine Tomatoes,
½ Cucumber,
Handful of Mint,
Small Handful of Rocket (optional),
1 Tbsp. White Wine Vinegar,
Lemon Wedges to serve.

For the Pickled Sultanas;

200g Sultanas,
150ml Water,
100ml White Wine Vinegar,
2 Tbsp. White Sugar,
2 tsp. Mustard Seeds,
1 tsp. Whole Black Peppercorns,
1 tsp. Dijon Mustard,
1 Bay Leaf.

Method;

Pickle preparation several days ahead is simple. In a saucepan combine all of the ingredients listed, start with the dry ones before adding any liquid. Raise to a simmer for 10-15 minutes and then decant all of it into a sterilised jar (sterilisation is usually done with a large quantity of boiling water). After 2/3 days the sultanas should have taken on the pickle and are ready to use.

The buckwheat can be prepared ahead of time although this is not essential. Rinse the grains and boil them in plenty of water until completely tender. Skim off any dirt or foam that forms on the surface of the water. Or, soak overnight or until soft, changing the water once. To prepare the salad find a large bowl and combine the buckwheat, three handfuls of pickled sultanas (do not worry if a little of the liquid makes it across but try to ovoid the pickling spices other than mustard seeds – whole peppercorns are particularly odious to bite into). Thinly slice the radish into rounds, rough chopped the mint and add these and the oregano also. The cucumber should be sliced in half lengthways and its wet centre removed before chopping into crescent moon shapes. The tomato must be treated in a similar vein; it should be quartered and its core should be removed before cutting into long thin juliennes. Drizzle over the vinegar and a little olive oil. Season enthusiastically with salt and pepper and mix all ingredients together. Serve generous portions with a lemon slice and a scattering of leaves.

French Bean Salad with Toasted Almonds and Soft-Boiled Egg.

If there was any time to pull out the truffle oil it may be now. However, as a staunch non-believer I cannot condone its use at any time. The stuff should be burnt. Any gastro-pub that has succeeded in 'keeping up with the times' so much that is whiffs no longer of cigarettes but rather of truffle should be closed down by the ombudsman. Here accept a humble bean and egg salad; toasted almond flakes can be bought, but they usually come without tasting of almonds. This negates their purpose. Toasting your own is easy and will also result in a deep burnt yellow hue rather than a white one – more homely. If you are a chemistry enthusiast, biology teacher or incredibly keen chef you will own a water bath. These can be used to poach eggs in the shell, which produced a more perfect egg, poach the eggs in the shell at 62.5*c for one hour if you wish to use this method.

Ingredients;

350g French Beans,
4 Large Eggs,
100g Almonds,

2 Tbsp. Wholegrain Mustard,
1 Tbsp. Dijon Mustard.

Method;

Blanche the green beans by the same method as the asparagus on page. 36. by preparing a large pan of boiling water and blanching the spears in the water for 1-2 minutes; it is important to retain some bite. Remove from the pan and immediately refresh in ice cold water. The eggs may also be pre-prepared as they should be allowed to cool. Soft boiling usually takes 3-4 minutes, the timing begins after the water starts to re-boil after the eggs are added. They also may be stored in the fridge but both elements should be removed an hour before being eaten in order to come back to room temperature. When this is done, toast the almonds in a dry salted pan and then crush them into small chunks in a bag. Combine beans, some of the almonds, mustards, and a healthy swig of oil with salt and pepper and toss them all until mixed thoroughly. When serving top a pile of beans with one egg, shell removed, which will release its golden runny yolk on impact. Top with a sprinkling of extra toasted almonds.

Marinated Halloumi with Salsa Verde.

Finally, the two best things in the world in one place. The Spanish are known for being incredibly imaginative and this is no exception, 'Salsa Verde', translates directly as 'green sauce'. Which is not a lie. Salsa Verde is the best type of sauce in the world, it is not a thing in itself but rather a group of green sauces that are made without cooking. Pesto, the godly chimichurri sauce and many other snotty concoctions that one could invent are all Verde salsas. Grilled halloumi, well, nothing needs to be said about that. Marinating, although time consuming, bears fruitful results and can even make cooking easier when the time comes. Additionally, the halloumi here will arrive in front of the BBQ or blowtorch already sliced which saving a lot of pratting around when it's time to eat. This one makes for a good starter or tapas like dish in a wider collection, but I am sure you get the idea by now, welcome to the end of the first section. I hope you are still hungry.

Ingredients;

500g Quality Halloumi,
300ml Olive Oil,
90g Capers,
50ml White Wine Vinegar,
1 Shallot,
6 Garlic Cloves,

2 Dried Chillies,
Handful Fresh Coriander,
Smaller Handful of Fresh Parsley,
Small Handful of Oregano,
1 Lemon,
1 tsp. Sugar.

Method;

Slice the Halloumi with a sharp clean knife, trying to avoid breakage, into large triangles. Cut diagonally in half and then slice each wedge into four by continually halving. This way each block produces 8 triangles. In a tub or baking dish combine 200ml of olive oil, four garlic cloves and the two dried chillies – chopped finely. Zest the lemon, add this zest and a squeeze of juice. It would be possible to add anything to the marinade but as this will be served with a strong sauce, unnecessary. Leave these feta icebergs floating in the sea of oil for a few hours; turning them occasionally if you have the chance.

Mix the remaining ingredients to make the 'green sauce' closer to serving. The shallot and garlic should be diced and herbs roughly chopped. Combine the ingredients a bowl with the oil, vinegar, capers, sugar, salt and another squeeze of lemon juice. Beware of adding too much oil, if the sauce appears wet incorporate more fresh herbs. When serving, the halloumi may be blowtorched until brown of grilled on a BBQ or grill-plate. Dollop the herby dip over the halloumi which, in triangles, can be attractively stacked.

Repas;

The 'main' section of this collection contains recipes for dishes that for one reason or another it would be considered normal to eat alone and in larger quantities than those listed above. The separation is only a formality and should not be taken too seriously. Indeed, in Italy, although this is not the nation in question, pasta dishes (several of which are shortly to come) are usually eaten first.

It may have already become obvious that I personally believe all foods benefit from being served with a small leafy salad. This is especially true of the forthcoming meals and will probably be stated even more in the following pages than it already has been. Adding more ingredients, especially if they are vitamin and nutrient rich ones is good practice when complimentary flavours are involved. Add substance and individual flare to a recipe when possible. There being more to eat is rarely a problem if it's this good.

I am a fan of Escoffier's ethos, *'faites sample'*, when it comes to mains and aim to cook the largest meals with the smallest possible quantity of pans or baking trays. This saves time, focuses attention and minimises opportunity for flavours to escape. Of course, it is not always possible and the man himself certainly didn't heed his own advice. Still, do not expect to be given the challenge of simultaneously managing the cooking of three frying pans, a saucepan, grill, two oven trays, a BBQ, blender and a rice cooker. This is cooking for the home, and the friends, not for show or expensive guests. Do try to keep good eyes on what instruction that is given though; a flustered host is never cool.

Menu

Pesto Steak Tartare.

A tartare is a binding of incredibly fresh raw beef, vegetables and seasonings – topped with an egg yolk. The most important ingredient, the beef, must have the perfect flavour as it will remain completely unaltered by the effects of cooking. High quality tenderloin cuts such as Fillet-Mignon or chateaubriand are best; if this cannot be found look for those with less fat and sinew as these will ruin the texture. Research carefully and talk to a butcher. This twist on the classic steak tartare is certainly one of the finest things I have ever eaten in France, it was earlier in the year, in the Cote d'Azur hill town of Eze. I did not ask for the recipe, the bistro was so busy we were gifted free shots to compensate for holes in the service, there were two results. Firstly, the 427m hill path descent to Eze-Sur-Mer passed incredibly easily. But more critically, I would have to replicate the tartare by memory – back in the UK. The dish should be served with chips and salad. It benefits from being eaten with other things as being so lightweight it acts almost as a sauce.

Ingredients;

2 Small Fillets of High Quality Steak,
2 Large Handfuls of Basil Leaves,
50g Pecorino Romano (Mild),
25g Capers,
20ml Olive Oil,
2 Egg Yolks,
2 Shallots,

Small Bunch of Chives,
2 tsp. Tabasco Sauce (As mentioned previously this is not for spice but depth),
2 tsp. Worcester Sauce,

Mixed Salad Leaves, Cherry Tomatoes and Balsamic Glaze to serve.

Method;

To prepare the best tartare chill the beef and mixing bowl in the freezer for 15 minutes. This is the best way to make the meat easy to chop into the small pieces it must become – without using a meat grinder. After this time the beef should be firm but not frozen. Slice each steak very thinly and then working on a perpendicular slice thinly again to create small strands of beef. This does not have to be neat but having evenly sized chunks is necessary. Drop these pieces back into the chilled mixing bowl and combine with the seasonings and oil. Shallots should be diced finely, capers halved, and herbs chopped small. (Retain several chive spears, these will be cut into finger lengths, to decorate at the end). Crack and separate the egg; add the yolk to the bowl and store the white for other recipes. I usually incorporate the yolk into the tartare here, but you may wish to serve it on top.

Mix all of these ingredients together thoroughly with a little salt and pepper before adding the cheese as it will break easily. For this recipe Pecorino Romano is best made into small paper-thin squares, this can be done by chopping off a correctly sized cuboid from the block and slicing it sideways with a very sharp knife. Gently incorporate the cheese and check the meat is fully defrosted; it should be by this time, but if not allow it to stand without warming completely up to room temperature. To serve, stuff the tartare mix into deep cookie-cutter rings to make stable tians – the rings will need to be slightly larger than the fillets originally were. Serve with salad, possibly also chips, decorate with herbs and some balsamic glaze.

Harissa Mussel Pappardelle.

This rich and pasta dish is inspired by the work of a talented Israeli-English chef who has become such a household name in the last few years that it is not necessary to specify who he is. However, a recipe is never complete, and here, with some alteration a good recipe idea is transformed into a fully-fledged exhortation of seafood pasta. This dish is to me a taste of comfort, home, and an easy excuse to splash out on harissa paste. Pappardelle is a very wide and flat variety of pasta, which can make for difficult eating, this does in some way add to the experience though. If it cannot be found, fresh or par-cooked lasagne sheets sliced lengthways produce the same effect. The other key ingredient, mussels, are best fresh - these are not difficult to find. Here we include half live, in shells, and half from a packet. This is obviously counterintuitive when aiming for all fresh ingredients it will however make for easier eating and more presentable plates. As a very rich pasta this meal is better eaten later in the evening as the stars begin to appear with red wine. It is practically inedible in the heat of the day.

Ingredients;

400g Washed and De-bearded Mussels in Shell,
200g Cooked Mussels,
500g Pappardelle Pasta,
400g Cherry Tomatoes,
100g Chorizo.
1 Large Onion,
2 Garlic Cloves,

150g Pitted Black Olives,
Large Handful of Parsley,
3 Tbsp. Harissa Paste,
2 tsp. *Piment d'Espelette* (A spice common to the French, the closest alternative in the UK is Hot Paprika),

150g Greek Yoghurt to serve.

Method;

Chop the onions into chunky rings, halve the cherry tomatoes and crush the garlic cloves. The chorizo and olives should be cut into rings and the parsley roughly chopped. This preparation allows for ease of cooking; time savvy cooks will be able to chop rapidly while going along – but why bother. With a little oil drop the onions and chorizo into the pan, the sausage will release some oil and colour of its own. Add cherry tomatoes, garlic, olives and shelled mussels shortly after when the onion begins to soften – put a lid on the pan to build the temperature. While the mussels cook prepare a large saucepan of boiling water for the pasta, with a dash of oil and salt. Checking the mussels will reveal some starting to open. As soon as the majority are visible add in the rest of the unshelled molluscs with the harissa, Piment d'espelette, a small amount of parsley and season with salt and pepper. Stir to ensure everything is coated with sauce. Heat on high for several minutes if the unshelled mussels need to be cooked and then drop to a simmer with the lid ajar. The pasta should be cooked until al dente which will not take long. As soon as it is drained cover in lashings of olive oil. One may toss the pasta and sauce together or leave them separately; the pappardelle will hold the sauce quite well if tossed over low heat. Serve in large pasta bowls and ensure each plate has several shelled mussels. Top with yoghurt and the remaining parsley.

Prawn and Snail Risotto.

It may seem fiendishly pompous but the inclusion of snails here originates from little more than the fact they were in the fridge. It is not an attempt to complicate a recipe for the sake of originality but rather a way consume some lumps of protein that were frankly not very enjoyable on their own. In French supermarkets snails are often sold frozen, pre-prepared, and stuffed with garlic butter. For some unknown reason it was decided that these mass-produced frozen snails would be the ones to go for. My limited experience with *escargot* means I cannot really comment on the quality of the product (I assume it was low) but never has a snail appealed to me anyway. Alone, with their garlic and herb butter, these were no exception. However, cooked again with other ingredients and eaten as part of a risotto the snails were reborn. In the UK obviously finding snails in the shops is almost impossible, which is good in my opinion, if you are willing seek some out, try them in this way, you may be surprised. I used a fish stock that had been prepared from the remains of fish filleted the night before; these are also available from a packet but I would advise anyone serious about eating to store scraps and off cuts in order to regularly make stocks.

Ingredients;

400g Arborio Risotto Rice,
A Troupe of Prawns,
A Hood of Snails,
1 White Onion,
125g Cherry Tomatoes,
Two Handfuls of Frozen Peas,
1/4 Tin of Chopped Tomatoes,
150g Butter,

½ Bulb of Garlic,
Fish Stock (made up with 1 litre of boiling water),
125ml White Wine, or, Lager,
2 Tbsp. White Wine Vinegar,
1 Tbsp. Tomato Puree,
2 tsp. Chilli Powder,
Boquet Garni.

Method;

Making the risotto will require two pans, one a very large skillet and the other a saucepan for keeping the stock warm. Start by dicing and softening the onion with some butter. In the saucepan heat up the fish stock or dissolve the stock cube. Add salt and pepper and any off cuts or peelings made in the rest of the cooking process – it all helps.

Chop the garlic and tomatoes, add these to the risotto pan when the onions are beginning to brown. Use more butter when required. Next add the meat, with the prawns peeled and de-strung if they are not already, along with the chilli powder and white wine vinegar. When the prawns are almost completely orange the rice may be added, dry at first, stir. After two minutes add chopped tomatoes, tomato puree with the white wine, a splash of stock and the *bouquet* of herbs. Stir so that the liquid is absorbed, when this happens add more stock and continue to stir. Add the frozen peas. Repeat the process until the rice is cooked soft and the whole mix is creamy and moist. A small amount of leftover stock is not a problem. Any remaining butter can be left on top to melt into the risotto. The *bouquet garni* should be found and placed on top where it is visible and the skillet served in the centre of the table with a serving spoon. *Bon appetit*!

Saffron and Chilli Scallop Spaghetti.

Seafood is not the only thing to eat but at the start of summer nothing suits better than some lightweight *fuits de mer*. If you are not a fan, this particularly precious pasta may change your orientation. Saffron, despite its reputation, really isn't that expensive and should be used generously. Its sensual aroma is completely intoxicating. So precious an aroma that puritan diners may wish to savour their saffron by excluding the latter two spices, this is fine, they should only be used in very small amounts anyway. Recently, I have collected an immense collection of old dried up birds eye chillies on a string; these are perfect for when 'crushed chillies' are required. They make the kitchen look colourful, are damn spicy, and are so dry that they may be crumbled between the fingers into or on the food for easy spice. Wash your hands afterwards. Should it be necessary to the occasion, the scallops may be served without pasta, whole but with the same sauce. Either way, the colour of this sauce is important. Make sure the pan used is clean and clear of all burnt matter. In other recipes this is often not so important and can even add to a dish. Many chinese chefs will not wash several of their woks in order to maintain the taste of 'wok chi', 'the air of the wok', which seems quite beautiful. But here it is.

Ingredients;

500g Dried Spaghetti,
12 Sea Scallops (this is three each; adjust as required),
100g Butter,
2 Shallots,
1500ml Double Cream,
100ml White Wine,

1 Medium Tomato,
Handful of Parsley,
Pinch of Saffron threads,
2 tsp. Chilli Flakes,
½ tsp. Turmeric,
1 Garlic Clove.

Method;

Prepare a saucepan of boiling water for the pasta, this should contain salt and a dash of olive oil. Cooking the spaghetti can be done before or during. Either way, boil until al dente (slightly more firm than usual as the pasta will heat more in the sauce). Drain and rest until needed.

Dice the shallots and garlic. Cut the tomato into cubes by quartering, removing the cores and cutting small cubes from the flattened outer flesh. The scallops should be sliced gently, with a good knife, into thin flat circles. I recommend three from each; it makes them incorporate more easily into the pasta. In a large frying pan melt half the butter until it is starting to foam, fry the tomato cubes, half the shallots and sear the scallops. Season lightly with salt and chilli. When the scallops are white and taking on small marks of cooking remove from the heat into a bowl, they should still be incredibly soft to the bite. In the same pan, melt the rest of the butter and fry the rest of the shallots and the garlic. A dash of white wine may be added to deglaze the pan but it is not essential. Add cream and all the other listed seasonings. Black pepper and fresh parsley are only to go on top of the dish however, as they may dull the colour if cooked into the saffron sauce. Adjust the heat of the frying pan accordingly to maintain a steady stream of small bubbles; the sauce will start to thicken as one continues to stir. It should take a strong yellow hue. Taste and season, more salt may be needed, if the spice flavours come on to the palette very late consider adding a touch of paprika or a different chilli powder as this should even out the flavour's distribution. When the flavour is rich and the sauce slightly thickened add the spaghetti and allow in to warm back up. Re-introduce the scallops as well. When Serving, try to place some of the scallop discs on top of the pasta. Garnish with herbs and pepper.

Ratatouille.

This is absolutely an *assiette* but listed here because it is my understanding the French eat it usually as a meal in itself. There are also rumours of Rat sandwiches; I think this is a great idea. Though we may have mastered the Yorkshire pudding and dipping bread into liquid cheese, which we consider to be French too, it seems that the British have never grasped the idea of eating something – with bread – in the same way other peoples do. This is certainly how the French consume their *ratatouille*, and it should be followed. See the recipe for baguette traditional on page. 18. There are two ways to make this dish; the proper way, and the way that makes it look like a piece of modern art. We know which is correct as the word, '*Ratatouille*', like this book, originates in the Occitan region and means 'to stir'. Stirring is not something you can do in the oven - it results in more of a stew than the rainbow coloured swirl of an ammonite. Both are acceptable, it depends who is eating and if the dish is indeed a main or an addition.

Ingredients;

2 Beef tomatoes (Or several smaller ones),
1 Aubergine,
1 Courgette,
1 Green Bell Pepper,
1 Yellow Bell Pepper,
1 White Onion,
½ Bulb of Garlic,

1 Tbsp. Tomato Puree,
2 tsp. Soy Sauce,
Handful of Basil,
Bouquet Garni (Rosemary and Thyme are essential),
Bay Leaf,
A splash of the evenings Red Wine,
Bread to Serve.

Method;

Really the tomatoes should be blanched to remove their skin, this is done by cutting a cross in the base before plunging into boiling water for thirty seconds, after this the skin is easily peeled off. They are chopped afterwards. Some may deem this unnecessary; you are welcome to decide. Another trick, equally optional, is to pour table salt over the Aubergine and courgette so as to reduce the bitterness of them. It is easier, and quite adequate to just peel off half of their skins. This can be done without boiling.

Either way, dice the tomatoes and roughly chop all the other vegetables into bits of equal size. The onions should be smaller, in lengths, and the garlic crushed. Now, work is done, drop the whole lot in the largest frying pan around. Layer the vegetables so that they cook correctly. Onions and garlic first, Aubergines, courgettes and peppers next. Tomatoes, bouquet and seasonings nestle on the top. The basil can wait.

Cook on a medium heat – just enough to hear the onions. For a while it is not necessary to stir, contrary to what was said before, both vegetables and meat appreciate being allowed to cook in their own time. When things are visibly softer stirring can begin, be kind, after a while place the basil leaves on the top. Let them wilt and stir them in too. Consider adding more salt and a splash more of wine. Everyone who wants to eat should be given some responsibility to stir – multiple stirring techniques combined will ensure nothing goes unstirred. The pan should simmer for at least an hour. It is cooked when you can smell it from the other room. Serve in the pan with bread, cheese and wine.

Beetroot Rainbow Salad with Lamb Kebabs.

This is a great one to prepare ahead of time for an easy BBQ treat as both parts must be left in the fridge for a while before serving. The recipe is packed with good things such as nutrients, and even better ones like sourness and salt. When packaged up in the to go section of a supermarket, salads like these usually receive the title 'detox' or 'revitalise', such labels are obviously to entice health crazed millennial shoppers - but they are not all lies. One usually feels better after eating this salad and the high fibre content has obvious benefits for 'normalising' the digestive system after a long week drinking boxed French wine. Although kebab skewers are practical for cooking on a BBQ, and the idea of a meat lollipop is hilarious, this touch is not an essential. Balls of seasoned lamb may be cooked in many ways and incorporated into the salad before serving. Baby leaf kale is used here, although full-grown adult kale can be, if the stiff stems are be removed and the salad is left to mull for slightly longer in the fridge.

Ingredients;

For the Kebabs;

750g Lamb Mince (high fat content mince is good for flavour and moistness),
1 Red Onion,
½ Bulb of Garlic,
Large Handful Coriander,
Small Handful Mint,
2 Handfuls of Pine Nuts,
Zest of One Lime (the juice of the lime may be used for the salad),
1 Birds Eye Chilli,
2 tsp. Cumin,
2 tsp. Coriander Seeds,
1 tsp. Fenugreek,
1 Sprigs of Thyme.

For the Salad;

300g Baby Leaf Kale
150g Green lentils,
4/5 Cooked Chilli Beetroot (If this is not available allow the beetroot to sit for a while in chopped fresh chillies and garlic before use),
3 Large Carrots,
2 Avocados,
1 Red Onion,
2 Limes.

Method;

Dry roast the seeds and nuts in a frying pan continually tossing and stirring until they are toasted and begin to jump around by themselves. Move to a pestle and mortar and grind into a powder. In a large bowl combine this with all the other ingredients which should be finely diced, or to save time, blended together in a food processor into small lumps. Thoroughly mix the lamb with these ingredients, using a generous amount of salt. Kebabs can be shaped by hand or rolled using a sheet of greaseproof paper. To do this cut a large sheet place and place it on the surface. Take a handful of the mince and roll it into a sausage between two layers of the folded paper. Insert skewers and place in the fridge for several hours before using as this will make them firmer. When the salad is also prepared and chilled cook under or above a gril or BBQ until slightly crisp.

For the salad, which also must be left in the fridge for several hours for the kale to soften, all ingredients are simply prepared and combined. Cook the lentils by boiling a pan of water three times the volume of the lentils, soaking the lentils is optional but they should certainly be rinsed before being cooked. After they are added to the boiling water reduce the temperature to a simmer and cook until the lentils are tender – drain them and rinse under running cold water to cool. wash and dry the kale, using a grater or vegetable peeler make the carrots to ribbons and use a knife to create thin matchsticks of beetroot. The above ingredients are stronger than avocado and should be combined and stirred in a large bowl with the juice of two limes, salt, pepper and olive oil before the avocado is added to avoid damaging it. The salad should look fresh and vibrant, after sitting covered in the fridge for an hour or more the vegetables will soften, and the colour spread throughout. The carrots and onions are particularly amazing when treated like this.

Mediterranean Grilled Vegetable Tart.

The French translation is of course *Tarte* but there seems to be little distinction between this and a pie, other than the latter sounding less appetising and in fact rather northern, I suppose that this choice depends entirely on what the pastry itself identifies as. The tart is however certainly not a quiche, but it could be, if you are fond of eggs. In creating this dish, a low-fat electrical countertop grill was used, this creating rather attractive dark grill lines on all our veggies. Although, if boxing is not your favourite sport, you may wish to grill in the oven or using a griddle plate over the hob which will work just the same. Once again, pre-made pastry is listed; if you are capable (I am not to be trusted with pastry) create your own, as I am sure it will improve the result. Of course, a small leafy salad is the recommended accompaniment for this dish. Leave the tart to do most of the talking, it has plenty to say, but it will not shout.

Ingredients;

1 Block Puff Pastry (Usually Jus-roll, gluten free varieties are available, but I cannot speak for their quality as a substitute),
150ml Milk,
100g Cheddar Cheese,
50g Plain Flour,
2 Bell Peppers (Green and yellow are best).

2 Medium Vine Tomatoes,
1 Courgette,
1 Red Onion,
Rosemary Sprigs,
½ Bulb of Garlic,
50g Plain Flour,
1 Bay Leaf.

Method;

Tomatoes and Courgettes must be cut into rounds, the pepper should be rough chopped into squares, and the onion quartered and then deconstructed into what should be triangular layers. If more pages and specific terminology were available this chopping would be easier to explain – readers will have to engage their imaginations. All of these, except the tomato, need to be pre-grilled. They may remain slightly undercooked at this point but should take on some colour (grill lines if your equipment permits). Once this is done set them aside. On a floured surface roll out the pastry to a reasonable thickness, around one cm, and to the shape of whatever dish will be used. Throughout the process it should be lifted and turned to prevent sticking. This particular pastry brand instructs greasing the dish with oil, so follow individual packet instructions when putting it into the dish.

Heat a fan oven to 180*c. In the saucepan on the hob a cheese and garlic *béchamel* is to be made. Over fairly low heat combine the milk and flour while whisking with vigour. Add finely chopped or pasted garlic (eager chefs really should first boil the garlic alone as whole cloves to remove bitterness), the bay leaf and a sprig of rosemary, season with salt. It is necessary to whisk quite a lot but it will become clear when the sauce is starting to thicken – remove the bay and rosemary. When this happens, the cheese may be steadily added (a handful should be retained), it will incorporate easily into the sauce. Put the grilled vegetables into the pastry lined dish and top with the tomato slices. Neatness is not necessary but aim for an even distribution of each vegetable variety - crack black pepper on top. Over this arrangement the sauce may be poured, if your tray is not dissimilar to mine, the levels of vegetables and béchamel will roughly match. The remaining cheese is placed on top to create a firm skin. For aroma and decoration two more rosemary sprigs are added in the centre of the dish before it is put in the oven. The *tarte* is cooked when the pastry and surface both begin to brown.

Cider Marinated Pork Chops with Greek Salad.

Unfortunately there is no plan on the horizon for a book of Greek food. Even though I claim it to be one of my favourite cuisines there are simply too many other things to write about. For this reason, this meal will make it into the current collection. Greek history has influenced every aspect of western and now worldwide life and therefore by definition must have had some effect on the evolution of tastes that were jokingly described at the start of this work. This recipe came from my attempt to recreate one very Greek supper, eaten at a clifftop taverna, on the island of Cephalonia. Certainly one of the best things to ever touch my tongue. Dr Iannis, a fictional Cepehlonian, advocates gentlemen urinating on their garden herbs - In order to fertilize the soil. There may be some validity in the claim, but I assure my friends this practice has not been adopted in my own garden. It is certainly not recommended when visiting other people's homes. The meat needs several hours to marinate for best results, even a day, this can be done in either a baking tray or a plastic bag. Usually I avoid the bag, fearing plastic interfering with my marination, though this fear is probably unfounded, plastic is certainly used in professional cooking by means of vacuum bag. This meal is suited to a warm summer evening; as is always the weather in Greece, and occasionally France. The umami (savoury) is what makes it so good; a mountain of cool tzatziki and a brick of tangy cheese, balancing the lovingly marinated pork. Serve with a humble salad and wholesome pitta bread, possibly even salty chips if you find the time, umami is the only word to describe it. Pure satisfaction, worthy of a short lie down, will be reached.

Ingredients;

4 Thick Cut Pork Chops (6-8 smaller ones).
4 Pitta Breads,
200g Greek Feta,
1 Large Iceberg Lettuce,
3 Salad Tomatoes,
1 White Onion,
2/3 Pint of Strong Flat Cider,
150ml White Wine Vinegar,
2 Large Handfuls of Fresh Oregano,
4 Garlic Cloves,
Olive Oil, (Listed as it is required in a fair quantity).

For the Tzatziki;

500g Full Fat Greek Yoghurt,
1/2 Cucumber,
2 Handfuls of Mint,
Small Handful of Dill,
2 Tbsp. Lemon Juice,
1 Tbsp. Lemon Zest,
1 Garlic Clove.

Method;

Prepare the pork in a marinade. This is easily done in a large oven tray - the same one it will be cooked in. Drizzle a small amount of oil in the bottom of the tray and salt it generously. Roughly chop the oregano, removing most of the stems first, and slice the onions into half rounds. Place half the onions and half the oregano in the dish with the four cracked garlic cloves and put the chops on top of this. The other half of the onions and oregano can go on top. Pour over the cider and vinegar season with more salt and place in the fridge – covered. This should be left for the whole afternoon.

The only other preparation is combining the ingredients of the tzatziki which may also be done in advance. Shred or dice the cucumber, chop the mint, finely but with only one pass, crush the garlic clove and mix these in a bowl with the other ingredients listed. Season to taste with salt and pepper. Store until needed, covered, in the fridge. The pork should be cooked for around 45 minutes at 180*c, this time varies depending on the thickness of cut and the only way to know is to check the meat is not still pink.

To serve, toast the pitta breads and cut them open, slice the tomatoes into large rounds and the feta into thick wedges (this is how it was served to me). Tear the lettuce apart by hand and wash it. Drip the sauce from the pork over the salad as a dressing. This meal goes well with a communal dish of Kalamata olives and a plate of homemade chips.

Hard Fried Fish with Red Lentil Dahl.

A generously tall '*darne*' or '*troncon*' fillet is best here as they stand proud on the plate. These cuts are steaks cut straight through the spine. Their thickness permits 'hard' frying, harder than a fish is normally fried, whereby the outside may be crispy and the core still delicate. The names of these cuts are often used without clarity, the difference refers to if the fish used is a flat or round one. Both types are suitable if good cuts can be found. As Rick Stien noted; fish is wild food, and we must accept what is available, not dictate what we will eat. Appearing generous is the most important thing for a dish to do when it is served, taste and smell aside, but the importance of this trait is too often forgotten by restaurants. They often ignore nourishing and warming their clients and focus too much on making their dishes, starters and mains alike, into works of dainty, carefully balanced art. For me this is not what food should represent. I have put much thought into sauces for this fish but reached the conclusion that almost none is needed. With the dahl, quality fish needs very little extra - but a small coconut sauce does do the trick. The dahl here is my mothers, I used to hate it, but growing older have reasoned that it is actually one of the best things she showed me. It is the definition of warming, nourishing and generous food and would have been included on its own in the *assiettes* section if it had not proven such good accompaniment to fish.

Ingredients;

For the Dahl;
300g Red Lentils,
1 White Onion,
250ml Coconut Milk,
150g Cherry Tomatoes,
2 Garlic Cloves,
1 Tbsp. Turmeric,
1 Tbsp. Tomato Puree,
1 tsp. Paprika.

For the Sauce;
400ml Coconut Milk,
Small Handful Parsley,
2 tsp. Fish Sauce.

And;
4 *Troncon* Fillets of Fish,
Rapeseed Oil.

Method;

Begin with the dahl and sauce as these can be left on a low heat to stay warm while the fish is cooked. For the sauce find a frying pan and combine all the ingredients listed - retain half of the parsley for garnish. Simply heat at a simmer to reduce the sauce, stir occasionally, and season with salt.

For the Dahl dice the onion and fry in a saucepan with olive oil. Add the garlic, similarly chopped, when the onions soften slightly. Add the tomatoes, halved, and the puree with the spices and to the onions. Season with salt and pepper. Add the lentils and stir, then add boiling water, start with only slightly more water than the height of lentils. Turn the heat to a simmer. As the water is absorbed continue to replace it until the lentils are nearly cooked and only have a slight bite. Incorporate the coconut milk and stir some more. Check the taste and season appropriately. Use more turmeric to increase the yellow colour if necessary. Drop to a very low heat and cover with a lid. If the sauce has become thicker reduce the heat to a minimum and cover this also.

To fry the fish, heat a small depth of oil in a frying pan that will fit all four fillets. Fry on all sides for several minutes (on the skin mostly if you have this). Try to get a crisp outer layer. When it is cooked the fish will easily flake if pushed. This point will easily be reached by hard frying like this. Remove the fillets and place on a kitchen towel to drain the oil. Arrange the three elements on the plate – obviously topping the fish with the coconut sauce. Garnish with parsley and consider serving with an optional chilli sauce.

Steak Salad with Asian Dressing.

In the east, on a different branch of foods history, there are many reflections of the French cuisine. Consider the ingredients of this dish; I would personally think them very French. At least individually, even if they are not when combined in this way. A special addition to this plate is several dollops of chilli jam. The one I use adds sweetness, spice and moisture to the salad. This excellent recipe may be provided in the future but sadly wounds must first be properly healed with the recipe owner's daughter – for copyright reasons. If you are lucky enough to have a chilli jam, then it is not necessary to give such depth to the dressing. It may also be a good idea to use fewer chillies. As it goes, each person dining on this recipe will receive half a steak, if you have a good butcher (or juicy supermarket), this usually goes far enough. Using only one steak would make for a good four-person starter.

Ingredients;

For the Salad;

Two Large Rump Steaks,
4 Portions Mixed Leaf Salad,
150g Button Mushrooms,
150g Mangetout,
Large Handful of Coriander,
2 Shallots,
2 Tbsp. Butter,
1 Large Chilli,
Thumb of Ginger,
1 Garlic Clove.

For the Dressing;

2 Tbsp. Soy Sauce,
2 Tbsp. Olive Oil,
1 Tbsp. Red Wine Vinegar,
1 Tbsp. Lime juice,
1 Garlic Clove,
1 tsp. White Sugar,
1 tsp. Chilli Flakes,
½ tsp. Ground White Pepper.

Method;

Crush the garlic and combine with all the other ingredients of the dressing – this is best done in a jar or bottle, so it can be shaken, and stored.

Season the rumps with salt and pepper and fry in butter for 2 minutes 15 on each side. Remove from the pan and allow to cool. The mushrooms should be halved and the mangetout cut at 45* angles to create long sticks which often look funny when viewed in cross section. In the same pan, with more butter, fry the mushrooms and mangetout pieces with one cracked whole clove of garlic. This should not be done for very long at all, the mangetout should retain its bite. Slice the steak thinly as this will help it to cool more quickly before serving. If it has been cooked correctly the browned outside should only penetrate only a few millimetres into the meat. As a salad topping: roughly chop the coriander (stems removed), half-moon the shallots and chillies and cut the ginger into small matchsticks. Combine these three with a pinch of salt and mix together in a bowl. To construct the salad as I would, create a fan of steak slices on the plate and place a ball of salad in the centre. Cover with a serving of mangetout and mushrooms, which should have cooled slightly, and the shallot and coriander garnish and top generously with the 'Asian dressing'.

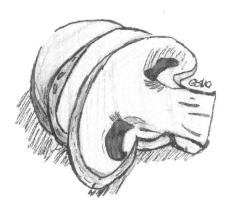

Sweets;

Not personally being a lover of the pastry section has affected, and limited, the choice of sweets given here. Pastry is of course an essential part of French cuisine and my introduction to it will not be a fair as my clumsy hands have never succeeded in replicating the delicate bakes of the *boulangerie*. Sugar and pastry are two of the most fragile things in the kitchen; they have to be treated with incredible care and attention. There is a time and a place for sweets: at the end of a meal, and at the end of a book. I would like to thank you now for coming so far, sitting through meals with the four of us, and I hope that some of these ideas will appear on your own table in the near future.

Menu

Tarte Tartin and Chantilly Cream.

Tarte Tartin;

This decadent desert first came to me via a friend who had been allowed to take leftovers home from work. It was more than two days old, wrapped in cling film and simply divine. One of the most impressive features of the recipe is a simple *tarte tartin* can be made for quite literally a couple of pounds; we have however recently investigated adding alcohol to the tarte - which slightly inflates the cost. This alteration will not be included here but I urge you to experiment. Rum, whiskey and even wine can be complimentary. The most playful aspect of the desert is that it is made upside down; although not everyone shares my amusement at this. The particular method given here saves a lot of messing around and washing up as the same frying pan holds the tarte from start to finish. Special *tartin* dishes are available, I assume to prevent the cooked caramel sticking, but they are not an essential.

Ingredients;

3 Red Eating Apples,	75g Brown Sugar,
1 Cooking Apple,	Thumb of Ginger,
1 Sheet of Puff Pastry,	3 Tbsp. Double Cream,
100g Butter,	1 tsp. Cinnamon.

Method;

Locate a large oven-proof frying pan and preheat the oven to 200*c. Start by quartering and coring the apples. If the cooking apple is significantly larger it may need to be cut into 5ths or 6ths to match the size of the other quarters. Make a caramel in the frying pan by melting the butter and adding the sugar with a splash of water. Raise the temperature to a fast simmer. The sugar will start darkening, stir slowly to make sure the colouration is even. Crush the ginger and add this with the cinnamon. When the caramel is formed reduce the heat to a minimum, add the cream, incorporate, and lay the first apple quarter, face down, in the caramel. Working clockwise, slightly overlap each quarter to build a full circle. Fill the centre with remaining quarters. They should all be almost fully submerged. Roll out the puff pastry until 2 cm thick, lay it tightly over the top of the pan and trim the edges. Poke holes in the centre with a fork and sprinkle with a small amount of extra sugar. Bake in the oven until the pastry is golden brown. When it is done tease the edges with a spatula to free the pastry. Flip the pan out onto a chopping board and slice with a clean knife. Serve with Chantilly, or ice cream.

Chantilly Cream;

This recipe is included as an accompaniment to the *tarte tartin* as I do not believe any host would be idiotic, or hilarious, enough to serve a bowl of whipped cream alone as a desert. Chantilly cream is however a staple of French pastry cooking and may be eaten with many other things too and thus must be included in this collection. It certainly goes well with the *tarte tartin* listed previously. A good electric whisk is helpful but adequate results may be achieved by hand with only minimal RSI. The cream may be kept for several days in the fridge and lasts even beyond the time it collapses if re-whipped back into life. Do not be shy with the flavourings, they will not bite. For an interesting variation, up to one quarter of the volume of cream used may be substituted with baileys and several pinches of ground instant coffee added to create a sweet and alcoholic coffee Chantilly.

Ingredients;

350ml Double Cream,
30g Caster Sugar,
4 tsp. Vanilla Extract.

Method;

In a mixing bowl or the bowl of electric whisk pour in the cream, reserving a small amount. Add in the sugar and vanilla this is after the cream to prevent them sticking to the sides. Whisk until stable peaks form, if the cream becomes too hard the remainder may be added and very briefly incorporated. Use in a piping bag to make serving more practical.

Figs Roties aux Mendiants et au Caramel Epice.

Pardon my French. The final note on figs will be a simple one, I am told these figs go excellently with a light ice-cream or some shortbread biscuits. Or of course as a treat – both. Working with sugar and sweets is very hard. That is why a pastry chef is to be respected and also why the sweets section of this collection is so short. Caramel is not the hardest; but it is worth paying attention to. Small temperature changes have large effects on the structures of sugars which causes them to be temperamental – literally. Hopefully one day fig trees will grow again at *les figues;* I suppose if somebody plants them, they will.

Ingredients;

4 Figs,

Small Bunch White Grapes,

Handful of Raspberries.

50g Sugar,

50g Butter,

25ml Tap Water,

Squeeze of Lemon Juice,

1/2 Tbsp. All-Spice,

1 tsp. Cinnamon (Or a small stick),

Method;

Rinse the fruits and chop into halves or quarters depending on size, leave the raspberries whole. Under a grill briefly roast the fruits under a sprinkling of sugar and salt. The figs, as the more stubborn fruit, benefit from being roasted for slightly longer. To make a caramel sauce place the sugar, water and lemon juice in a saucepan. Make sure the sugar forms an even layer over the entire base of the pan and does not stand in the middle. Allow this to boil steadily for a while until it darkens in colour to a light amber and thickens slightly. This will be a fairly rapid transition. At this point remove from the heat and stir in the spices and butter. The caramel will stay liquid if left un-refrigerated. It may handle the cold if it has be stored but should be allowed to reach room temperature before serving anyway. Heat gently to loosen if it will not pour. Serve by building a tower of fruits and pouring over some of the caramel sauce. Consider decorating with edible flowers.

Simple Cookies.

If there were a simplicity competition in which these cookies came head to head with a bowl of Chantilly cream the winner would be whoever's table the event took place on, because through their rivalry these two items would have created a lovely desert, rendering the whole contest pointless. Though both of these processes could easily be completed by an illiterate 9-year-old they are included because they are the basis for personal exploration. They were also made on our trip to France, not by me, but by a friend. There is of course no need to dismiss things because of their simplicity and often this trait is desirable, everyone enjoys a slightly chewy, slightly warm cookie. That's a fact. After the first tray had been cremated before even being born, and the second batch revealed themselves to contain around 50% bicarbonate of soda which creates a strange popping candy sensation on the tongue, we managed to create a perfectly simple cookie. Add broken bits of chocolate or even coffee if you want to liven things up a bit.

Ingredients;

300g Plain Flour,   1 tsp. Vanilla Extract,
220g Caster Sugar,   1 tsp. Baking Powder,
200g Butter,   1 tsp. Salt.
1 Egg,

Method;

Soften the butter and mix ingredients together, place cookie sized lumps on a tray covered in greaseproof paper, bake in the oven (180*c) until slightly crisp around the outside

Tequila and Lime Sorbet.

This has been a first attempt at making sorbet, I have ignored a great deal of the advice that is online, and I think it has still gone quite well. '*Faites Sample*' indeed. No 'ice cream machine' here, just will power, and an optional handheld electric whisk. No matter what equipment you have though, this is a long process, it should be started early in the morning. Ice creams and sorbets are some of the few deserts I really enjoy and this one really is just great. Unfortunately, for scientific reasons, one cannot use a great deal of tequila in the sorbet. It creates too many ice crystals in the finished product. Fear not however, the restrictions on frozen tequila will only increase the volume that can be consumed in the usual liquid fashion before or accompanying the sorbet itself. For those who like a game, try having one shot of tequila every time the sorbet is taken out of the freezer to be re-crushed. Good Luck!

Ingredients;

300ml Tequila,	4 Limes,
300ml Water,	1 Egg White.
300g Caster of Sugar,	Salt.

Method;

In a reasonable saucepan boil the water, the tequila, lime zest, lime juice and sugar together to dissolve the sugar – similarly to the start of the process of making caramel but not long enough for any colour change. Remove from the heat and allow to cool. In a large mixing bowl crack and separate the egg, whisk the white until it is a stiff foam. Incorporate the tequila and lime syrup. Whisk thoroughly again. If the bowl will fit, put the mix in the freezer. Otherwise, decant into another container. Freeze for two hours, this should be enough to almost fully solidify the mix. Crush slightly by hand with a blunt implement and then, using the whisk (which by this point is ideally an electric one), re-crush all the chunks of ice into the smoothest slush possible. Return it to the freezer and repeat the process every hour and a half until it starts to re-freeze looking like a sorbet not a block of ice. It will begin solidifying much faster and take on a smooth, silky appearance. This may take 6-8 repeats of the crushing process. After this is complete re-freezing is only to maintain the solidity of the sorbet, it can be used as normal. To serve, remove from the freezer until soft enough to be scooped and make perfect balls with an ice cream scoop in a margarita glass garnished with fresh lime and uncrushed sea salt.

Poached Pears.

This is the final recipe of the book, and rightly so, poached pears are a rich and aromatic desert best served late in the evening alongside ice cream and a potent alcoholic drink. Pyromaniacal cooks might consider serving a pear to the table on fire, by dowsing the dish itself in alcohol, however I consider this a waste. This particular *recette* may be one of the most French in the entire collection. It not only contains French red wine but is taken from the mind of one of my first chefs, a Frenchman, whose love and understanding of the foods of France and Britain continues to impress me.

Ingredients;

4 pears,
1 Bottle French Red Wine (Must be French, out of respect, but disrespectfully cheap),
2 Tbsp. White Sugar,
2 Tbsp. Cinnamon or Half a Cinnamon Stick,
Bay Leaf,
Sprig of Thyme,
2 Star Anise.

Method;

Peel the pears carefully, in long strokes from the top to the base, by holding the stalk. Use a paring knife to remove the black tip at the base but not the stalk. Combine the other ingredients in a saucepan large enough to accommodate the four pears and raise to a simmering temperature. Add the four pears and make sure they are all completely submerged. I recommend creating a cartouche, which is essentially a baking paper lid, to cover the surface of the liquid. This technique which belongs to the French culinary tradition greatly improves evenness and quality of cooking. Simmer for 20-30 minutes, less ripe pears will require longer, test by piercing the pears with a skewer to check if the centres are softened. Remove the pears but continue simmering the liquid portion until it reduces into a syrup. Both the pears and the syrup should be cooled and stored in a fridge – separately. When serving make several incisions through the wider bottom part of the pear so that it can be fanned out on the plate, top with the red wine syrup.

Acknowledgements.

I must thank many friends for their assistance in writing this book; for allowing me to bounce ideas off them and for helping to test all the recipes. Some with experience of cooking helped refine recipes and those talented with handling the written word helped push my work forward and kept me focused at times of difficulty. I thank individuals from France who have helped me speak more accurately about the food of their nation, and the people of Itzac who accepted us for a week in their village. Most importantly are those with whom I have worked with and learnt from over my short career in the kitchen. Chefs, if you notice things here that seem familiar, this is because when you showed these things to me, I was inspired to make them again. Writing this book has been difficult and taken a long time. It has been more an education for myself than anything else. One thing is still certain: I have still not finished my education.

Various cookbooks and guides have also informed my work that I would recommend anyone who has made it this far to read; these are:

David, E., 1950. Mediterranean food. London: John Lehman.
-            The first book picked from the shelf on arrival in Itzac, David is one of the most famous and most respected food writers in history, reading this tired paperback my views of both food and food writing were transformed. Several recipe elements or techniques I describe are based on her guidance.
Ottolenghi, Y., Wigley, T., and Howarth, E., 2018. Ottolenghi simple. London: Ebury.
-            Clearly one of the best cookbooks ever written and the source of an incredible dish, 'Pappardelle with rose harissa, black olives and capers', that sparked an idea for one similar recipe detailed above. There is no doubt pappardelle is the perfect pasta in both of these cases.
Nosrat, S., 2017. Salt, fat, acid, heat: the four elements of good cooking. New York: Simon & Schuster.
-            Nosrat's book and tv series are a friendly introduction to some important concepts in food; she aims as I do to encourage self awareness and experimentation in cooking.
Domine´ Andre´, Beer Gu¨nter, Schlagenhaufer, M., and Ditter, M., 2014. Culinaria France. Potsdam: Ullmann.
-            Culinaria France is a tour de force of research into regional specialities. After returning from the country is supported aspects of my research.
Goldstein, D., 2015. The Oxford companion to sugar and sweets. Oxford: Oxford University Press.
-
Rackleff, O. S., 1983. Escoffier, king of chefs. New York: Broadway Play. P.109.
-            Understanding Escoffier is key in seeing how French culinary traditions invaded the nations collective thoughts over the turn of the 20th century. Naturally something this work was concerned with.
Davidson, A., Jaine, T., and Vannithone, S., 2014. The Oxford companion to food. Oxford: Oxford University Press.
-            Used specifically here for the information on ratatouille and its origins but certainly a concise guide to all foods in a style most should strive to replicate. The oxford companions are almost as biblical as Elizabeth David's works.

I Love You All
—
James.

Printed in Poland
by Amazon Fulfillment
Poland Sp. z o.o., Wrocław

57794373R00061